Coffee House Job

Coffee House Job

E. Alex Riegelmann

Lionhead Press

lionheadpress.com

Photographer: Elizabeth Solano

Although the author and publisher have made every effort to ensure the accuracy and completeness of information contained in this work, we assume no responsibility for errors, inaccuracies, omissions, or any inconsistency herein. Any slights of people, places, or organizations are unintentional.

ISBN: 978-0-9892285-0-3

ATTENTION CORPORATIONS, UNIVERSITIES, COLLEGES, AND PROFESSIONAL ORGANIZATIONS: Quantity discounts are available on bulk purchases of this booklet for educational or gift purposes. Special books or book excerpts can also be created to fit specific needs. For information, please contact Lionhead Press, 7428 Amberly Drive, Colorado Springs, Colorado, 80923; ph 719-210-0296.

Table of Contents

Preface

When I was 16, I was hired at a coffee house in my neighborhood. It was hard work, and I didn't like it much—but I got to meet a lot of local people, and I made some money. It was a productive way to spend my evenings. But eventually, as it always does, life moved forward, and the little place went out of business. I ended up getting other jobs and going to school like other teenagers. Over the next five years, I thought little about working in that coffee house until, to my surprise, I ended up at another one.

By the time I was 21, I'd had better jobs, better luck, and more experience, but somehow I ended up at a coffee house again. This time, it was Starbucks, the world's biggest coffee chain, and it made me angry. I suppose you could say that I had my "quarter-life crisis." I felt like I was wasting my time there—like I was better than that job. I'd been working "better" jobs for years, yet there I was, at a coffee house, slinging espresso and washing dishes.

Upon starting at Starbucks, I noticed that almost everyone there had a certain mindset in common. They didn't like working there, but for the most part, they were giving it a good try. They were all dreamers, thinking of the next step in life—but not about where they were at that particular moment. Starbucks was their in-between place. The "current situation" they had to break out of somehow. Even people who had been there many years believed that it was temporary. Unimportant. Something to get out of the way so the real day could begin. The last thing they were focused on was enjoying being at Starbucks.

I was the same—except I was also pompous, self-righteous, and had an "I'm a starving artist" outlook on life. I did not feel like everyone else. I saw my coworkers as unenlightened wage-slaves. I saw customers as self-absorbed suburbanites. I saw my managers and superiors as nothing more than minions of the terrible and mighty oppressors of man. While I certainly thought of myself as a servant of a higher calling, momentarily sidetracked into this little job, that was the last thing I actually was. I had unknowingly (but completely) become the one thing I always hated: a hypocrite.

Over the course of several months, I became less happy and more tired every day. My constant question was: "When will this end?" It wasn't until I reached a breaking point, a crisis, that I began to consider why I might be at Starbucks. That maybe it wasn't a fluke or an accident. That maybe I wasn't being punished. That, maybe, there was something good to be had out of this job. Maybe the people there were part of something special. Maybe I was too. What would happen if I gave it my all, as few do? What if I came to work and saw it as my mission, as my responsibility, as if this coffee shop were mine, and my success or failure here was as important as the success or failure in my true passions or in my closest relationships?

Who would I be?

PART 1

Half a Heart

He who has a 'why' to live for can bear almost any 'how.'

Friedrich Nietzsche

One question—indeed, one word—can sum up the struggle of my life: "Why?"

I grew up a stubborn child. I questioned everything. School was a huge challenge for me because I refused to succeed at anything there weren't good reasons for. And that, for me, was almost everything. I sorely lacked motivation, which was a headache for teachers, my parents, and especially me.

I always wondered: Why should I work hard or seek out meaning in life when I have everything I need? I had enough to eat and activities to occupy my time. I could entertain myself for days with just a computer. If I wanted to see friends, we could always just hang out. My "purpose in life" was just a future thing.

I may not have voiced these thoughts, but my actions did. If I had been on fire with passion and felt strongly that I had a responsibility to the world I lived in, I wouldn't have dilly-dallied years away. The truth is, I had nothing to be passionate about while growing up. It had all been done. Changing the world is impossibly difficult, changing my habits was just not worth it, and besides, I was taught that "finding your passion" is just about finding a good job—which is *work*.

I am not alone. We are a whole generation asking, "Why?" That makes "Generation Why" a perfect name for us, doesn't it? *Working* seems to be all we know. No wonder we're not motivated. We have been taught that all we'll ever have is a *job* (so get a good one)! We have been educated to believe it's the most important choice in life. So, naturally, we see our young lives as a stage of preparation for our fabled "dream job." Our schooling. Our part-time work. Even our romantic relationships are seen as "practice" for that "one" we'll be married to.

Well, with all this preparation, it seems we're just waiting for life to start, aren't we? I know I was. *Preparation* has been the theme of my entire life. So, this is how I've lived—as if it's all just practice. Because if the game hasn't started yet, *then I don't have to show up.*

Last on My List

Prior to working at Starbucks, I had been hired at a startup software company in Dallas, Texas. This had been my best-paying job ever, and while I didn't make a ton of money, the fact that I was young, single, and living on my own meant that I was able to be financially independent and relatively worry-free. It was also a stay-at-home job, giving me even more freedom to manage my time and save money on travel expenses. There was even a Starbucks across the street from where I lived, giving me an alternative office whenever I wanted.

Yet, since I worked as a writer, I had a job only as long as there were things to write. So, as months went by and the company moved away from content development and more toward technical considerations, my job became less important, and before I knew it, I was being transferred into an "as-needed contractor" position. Which soon meant no work, and no money. So, I started to look for another job, confident that I would be able to find something easily with my experience. I was wrong.

News stations, technology firms, various magazines, newspapers... no one wanted to hire me. Over about three weeks, I threw resume after resume into the loop, and only a handful of replies came in. Finally, that last week, I had four job interviews lined up. Surely, I thought, one of these will come through for me. In fact, I might get multiple offers and therefore have a choice of jobs. By instinct, one of the applications I'd put in was to Starbucks. I thought it might make a good backup (it was already my other office, after all).

Well, my "backup" turned out to be the only gig that worked out. Everything else fell through. I was astonished that, despite all the applications and even a few interviews, a coffee house job was the only one I was able to get. A week earlier, I would have thought I was done with part-time retail and service industry jobs forever. I thought I was so well-qualified that I would surely find a new opportunity quickly. But with my savings ebbing away and no other leads, I had no choice; I took the job, not sure what to expect.

It started out well enough; I was the new guy, and I was okay with that. I learned how to make espresso, steam milk, and blend Frappuccinos. I wore a green apron like everyone else. It seemed fun at times, learning about different kinds of coffee and drinks. Yet I was always dismissive—I knew I would be moving on soon, so why work too hard? Those first days and weeks at work were tough, but I got through them by telling myself that it was just for a short time.

But as weeks passed by, my heart sank. I had no job leads, and I soon needed to pick up more and more work at Starbucks to pay bills—and almost immediately, my nonchalant attitude had negative consequences on my work. I was sloppy, and more often than not, if I completed a task, someone else would have to quietly step in and do it over again. It was humiliating, and I often went about my workday frustrated and restless as a result. These issues continued to build, and had me asking questions.

Why was I at Starbucks? Why was this happening to me? I had a good job before this. I had money. I could do what I wanted. Then suddenly I was poor and working constantly to pay bills. I didn't like people, so serving them coffee and being happy about it was a major drag. It was tough to get up in the morning. It was tougher still to have any energy. I was drained.

Furthermore, I'm not a very naturally social person. I love studying and discovering exciting new things, but I've always felt like other people held me back from this. So I wondered: how could Starbucks be something I was supposed to do with my time? Or anyone's, really? It wasn't just me. My coworkers were intelligent, talented people—also working at Starbucks. I looked at my situation and believed it was a meaningless, stupid, boring, exhausting, and pitiful waste of anyone's time.

I played the blame game, too. It's easy to find fault with whichever society you live in—and, boy, did I enjoy a good pity-party about how the United States abuses its citizens.

I usually blame the education system for the way we all turn out and for how we get stuck in places we don't want to be. It's easy to avoid responsibility when there's so much wrong around you. It's not *my* fault that the world is such a terrible place. Right?

As my stress and unanswered questions mounted, searching for other jobs began to take over my free time. I didn't really do much else. I wanted out. I applied to place after place, searching and searching for a new opportunity, but nothing came. My initial easygoing denial seethed into a confused anger.

...I'd Have to Do it for Everyone

About two months in, I was still not connected to my coworkers. I hadn't really made any friends, and my presence made them nervous. Because I was so irritable, I snapped at people who asked me to do the smallest tasks and haughtily refused help doing things I still didn't know how to do correctly.

I was not alone in my negative presence there. I noticed, both at my store and at others, that there were some employees with the same attitude. They, like me, saw their situation as a temporary "sentence" and were angry or depressed that it wasn't over yet. Coming to work was just a burden of life, like a painful chronic disease.

Though I had gotten better at the job, I was certainly still not exceptional at it. If I could cut corners, and no one would know, then I would do it in a heartbeat. Being so focused on myself, it was impossible to do a great job.

Why this elitist mindset? I saw myself as just "passing through" this place. Since I figured that Starbucks was a temporary situation (or maybe a simple mistake on my part), naturally I shouldn't have to invest too much of myself in it. But as it got harder and harder to bear, I continued to wonder: What am I doing here? Why am I being punished? Why the humiliation of being a barista? The answers didn't seem to be coming in.

Always ringing through my mind were the words: I'm better than this. I was furious, and it showed. I heard murmurs among coworkers of my "anger issues." Looking back, it makes sense that they felt that way; I came to work every day with only one thing on my mind: getting it done and getting out.

One day, I was working at the front register as a long line of people stood waiting to order. When it was his turn, a middle-aged man in ragged, dirty clothes walked up to me.

"Hey," he said, "I wanted to get a grande latte, but I only have two dollars. I'm sorry, but I don't have any other money with me. Can I still get it?" He appeared to be down on his luck, if not homeless. It was early morning during the dead of winter, so it was freezing cold outside. And if you've ever ordered a latte at Starbucks of the "grande" variety (it just means medium-sized), you know that, even if made plain, it costs well over two dollars.

Yet I looked at him and felt no remorse. "Sorry sir, I can't do that. If I give you this for free, I'd have to do it for everyone. Sorry," I replied. But I wasn't sorry. I was annoyed. If someone couldn't pay, then they shouldn't be there, I thought. Go to a cheaper coffee house. Besides, I had a point: If I gave this guy a free latte, then I'd have to give one to everyone in line—and they could all hear me.

Oh, the arrogance! I remember wondering why people were giving me strange looks, though now it's obvious: Giving away a drink for free happens all the time at Starbucks. It happens to be a generous company; placing people first and sales second is actually one of the company's core values. It was I who was hard-hearted and had the selfish pride to deny someone a simple cup of coffee. Why would I do that?

I have no one to blame but myself. I was sulking. I was projecting my own pain onto that person (who undoubtedly had enough to deal with): the pain that is the result of a self-centered outlook on life; pain that a person feels when they long for something greater than what they have, but don't appreciate what they *do* have.

PART 2

Bitterness

My generation is having its midlife crisis in its 20s.

Edward Norton

*E*ventually, you reach a breaking point. You realize you can't endure your life anymore. Either you have to change, or you have to escape. For me, this was the day that a coworker of mine (who we'll call "Ben") asked me to come into the back room so we could talk.

Ben and I had never really gotten along. We snapped at each other, and I always hated getting feedback from him. That day, we had worked in silence together as the tension built between us. He was mad at me, and frankly I was rather pissed at him as well. I walked into the back room, and he beckoned me to sit down.

He told me he thought I was being closed and unresponsive to feedback and that I was basically acting like an idiot. He was convinced that I regarded him and my other coworkers as fools. He seemed genuinely frustrated, and I could tell he didn't expect me to understand or to be receptive to what he was saying. There was tension in his posture and expression, as if he were bracing for a fight.

As much as I would have enjoyed tearing up the back room in a battle royale with Ben (using coffee spoodles as weapons, naturally), something about what he said rang true for me. I really was closed and unresponsive. In fact, I was anti-social. I didn't see my coworkers as equals, and as a result, I took direction very poorly—and worst of all, I treated them with less respect than they deserved. As he waited for me to answer, all of this rushed through my mind—and the more I realized I had been truly prideful and self-centered, the more it seemed like my entire world was turning over. Despite how much I disdained the person telling me this, I had to admit to the truth in his words.

So I did. I told him that I hadn't meant to create any tension, and I knew that I'd been hard-headed and tactless in my dealing with coworkers. I told him that I was trying to improve but that this type of job was different from what I was used to and was not a good fit for my personality. Finally, I apologized, acknowledging that there was no good excuse for the way I'd behaved.

As I spoke, I saw surprise in his eyes. When I finished, it was clear that he'd had no idea I would be receptive to what he said. He expected an argument... and astonishingly, he didn't get one. I first apologized to Ben, and then to another coworker I'd been rude to in the past. I realized that everyone there was in the same boat as I, and that they were also struggling to work through personal issues and troubles each day. It was at that time that something in me broke, as if some part of me had been holding up a great weight and could hold it no longer.

It was from that moment that everything changed. My pride was not worth the pain it was causing me, but it was especially not worth causing *others* more difficulty and stress.

A new chapter of working at Starbucks was beginning, and indeed, I had only just scratched the surface of the purpose behind my time there. It wasn't long before I knew that there was something special about it, that it wasn't an accident. If I was going to spend so much time there, a good percentage of my weekly life, then doing it half-heartedly was just choosing to suffer.

Turning Point

Growing up, I was a mostly unmotivated, unimpressed kid, losing myself in video games and fantasies that, to me, were better than real life. Writing, reading, and language were the only things I had shown a true interest or talent in, and this made my school career a lopsided affair. Because this caused me terrible difficulty, I had built up various methods for coping with having to go to a place I hated and to do things I didn't enjoy.

Similarly, at Starbucks—a place I hated going since I had to do things I didn't enjoy—I was coping. I was turning, once again, to pre-packaged entertainment to survive my days and nights. Games, movies, vacations. And then, when I had to be at work, I would give the bare minimum of effort required to keep the job. It was hourly income, so being a terrible employee didn't really affect whether I'd be paid. Showing up was enough.

As anyone who lives this type of life knows, it requires more than just maintaining—it requires constant *increase* to keep yourself going. I wasn't satisfied or happy with just a few hours of a new video game; I needed a whole day's worth of play to feel okay. Yet even then, I wanted more—something else.

I was lonely, so I wanted romance. I began searching for that, too. My life became a constant, roving search for a new fix. How could anyone blame me? I hated my job, which was where much of my energy was going. I'm a human being with human needs—was I not entitled to a fulfillment of those needs?

At least, that's what I thought. I tried to justify doing whatever I wanted—yet nothing I found was ever enough. Restlessness overtook me. I was always nervous, always thinking and moving too fast, because deep within myself, I was experiencing a starving hunger for something *greater* than the life I was living—leading me to do things I never thought I'd do.

What had I become? I felt like a shell—frighteningly weak and fragile, like the smallest extra pressure might cause me to shatter. I was depressed. What was I doing wrong? I'd had many jobs growing up, and more than a few were not exactly enjoyable, but this one felt the most hollow.

By the time Ben and I had that conversation in the back room, this had all reached a head. And I did shatter. I went home that night and realized how deeply negative I had been to my coworkers, and to people going into that Starbucks. It probably even affected the amount of business we got. I wasn't only displaying selfish behavior—I was a selfish person. I had only ever cared for myself, the whole time I'd worked at Starbucks! It's a wonder I wasn't fired. This wasn't at all who I wanted to be. It was not who I saw myself becoming in my early twenties. Yet, there I found myself: deep in a hole I had dug, *all while thinking I was going somewhere*.

That day, I felt like I'd let everyone (including myself) down, which was disappointing, but at the same time, it was freeing. I finally saw myself honestly. I realized that I wasn't different from anyone else. Sure, I had a different personality, but I was still just a man. I had the same needs, dreams, and struggles as other men. Furthermore, my actions affected other people, whether I knew it or not (and whether I wanted them to or not). I was not better than Starbucks, and never had been. In fact, it was a *mercy* that I was there. I had feeble people skills when I started that job, and Starbucks gave me a convenient outlet to work on them. Additionally, how could I expect to become some great writer unless I knew how to work hard? Starbucks was giving me a work ethic, if I chose to accept it. It was giving me skills I desperately needed, and I'd never acknowledged that.

I decided that I would not waste any more time being half-hearted at my coffee house job. So as I came to work and really put myself into it, as I washed dishes and swept floors *as best I honestly could*, I started to feel lighter. My burdens weren't needed at work, so I left them at home.

To my own amazement, talking to people became easier. Making lattes was easier, wiping out refrigerators was easier, selling coffee was just… easier. How on Earth had I done this any other way? I had been resisting being good at this. I was the one who wanted to be a terrible barista, all because my silly ego couldn't handle the implications of being a great one. So, I stopped fighting—I gave in. I gave in to the truth. Because honestly, I worked at Starbucks, honestly, I was *not* doing a good job, and honestly, I *could* be great at it. And *honestly*, there were no good reasons not to be.

It was time to live my life, and that life happened to be occurring at Starbucks, at home, and indeed, everywhere I went. I had been waiting for the life I really wanted to take me away from this place—but my "dream life" had been waiting for *me* to wake up and choose to live it. Perhaps I wasn't meant to work at a coffee house for the rest of my life, but the only way to move forward was to move my feet and boldly take the step I was given today.

PART 3

Caffeine

You give but a little when you give of your possessions.
It is when you give of yourself that you truly give.

Kahlil Gibran

Well, saying "work hard and your dreams will come true" is easy enough, but if you don't enjoy something, how do you give it 100%? Can you force yourself to do it despite how unpleasant it makes you feel?

Once, when I was a child, my dad made me clean our house gutters. He showed me how to do it and left me to the job, but I hated my life right about then. The entire exercise left me annoyed, and I did it as quickly as possible. Because we lived in a pine forest, the gutters were totally choked with needles. I half-heartedly did the job, leaving much of the "needle gunk" still clogging the gutters, so my dad made me go back and re-do it. Then I had to go back a third time. My father, needless to say, was not pleased.

Looking back, I realize that I wouldn't have been able to give that job 100% unless I truly loved my dad. Unless I cared about what was best for him. If I had, I would have cared about maintaining our house just as much as he did and would have done "chores" without being asked. My dad was always busy working on something, and if I'd done that job well, it probably would have really helped him out. But, since I saw it as a chore, I treated it as such.

Likewise, have you ever felt like you were trying your best, but you just didn't have the energy to really commit? That giving 100% was simply not doable? I have, many times, and used this to justify doing a mediocre job. I was missing the "juice," the energy, to do what I needed to do.

Then there are those people who seem to be able to do everything with zest, compassion, purpose, and drive. They always seem happy and elated to be wherever they are and are content with doing whatever they're doing. How do they do it?

Well, they love. They truly care about the people they're doing it for, so they make a conscious choice to place themselves in their work—to make whatever they're doing the most important thing right at that moment. As a result, they hold themselves accountable for their performance, they treat others the way they want to be treated, and they do everything with an inexplicable grace. We all know someone like this. They aren't perfect people, but they somehow inspire others by just being... themselves. They're able to love what they're doing today, despite its unpleasantness, precisely because the love they have for others makes their "job" more than just a job.

Even their dreams are fueled by the desire to help people. They're saving to adopt a child, or to start a business. They might have a passion for a field of study, but have to pay for college—and are willing to earn it. Or they're working to support their kids, whom they love more than life itself. They look forward and humbly accept that hard work, determination, and consistency will be required to achieve their dreams, which they also love. The only thing that sets them apart from anyone else is that they are *in love.*

Because they've fallen in love with something, their entire lives change. Actions born out of pride begin to melt away in these people's lives. A sense that they're a part of something greater than themselves comes upon them, and it's detectable.

These people are *servants.* It's hard to find a better word for what they do. They lift up those around them, and what they do is done well. Their time and energy literally serve the people and organizations that they're a part of, and they produce results that go beyond their personal gain and ripple beyond their immediate relationships.

Sometimes, servants start their own businesses, despite the risk and the fear of failure. Just as often, servants find that they really want to change something in the world. They see that people around them are hurting for one reason or another, and they resolve to change it. So, they set out to do just that, and despite naysayers, unjust laws, abandonment, and any number of terrible calamities, they never stop. How do they do it? *They're in love.*

It may sound cliché at first, but if you think about it, what could possibly pull someone through a difficult situation more surely than love? Look at mothers who get only a few hours of sleep every single night because they work a job, take their kids to football practice, grocery shop, cook food, clean their home, and do all else for their children. Only an *incredibly motivating force,* like love, could enable mothers to do this. They love their kids so much that providing for them feeds their own emotional and psychological needs and gives them the energy they need to keep doing it. Indeed, mothers and fathers who choose to love their kids with everything they have are the best of the bunch.

What I realized about love was that the people in my life deserved it—and that included all the people working at Starbucks, as well anyone that happened to come through there. I still didn't like washing dishes or mopping floors, and taking out trash is not exactly exciting—but what I could love were the people on both sides of the counter. Furthermore, coffee shops are places of introspection, conversation, creativity, and personal production, and maintaining and promoting those things was definitely worth my time. That made the small things worth doing, and doing well.

So I gave up my feelings of contempt and entitlement and accepted that the place I was in today was where I was supposed to be. Who was I to say that a coffee house job was a waste of time? I have so much to learn about life still. Maybe I was exactly where I was meant to be to start learning it. So, I went to work as if it were my responsibility. And when I did this, everything changed. *Everything.*

I was afraid that it was going to be too hard to sustain, but it wasn't any more difficult—and people noticed immediately. I was not well-liked at Starbucks, but no one could deny when I did a good job, or at least gave it my best shot. In a very short time, working there was much easier because most of the difficulty had been in being so alone, despite being surrounded by people.

Before long, my coworkers became friends. Where once I had considered them and me to be separate and incompatible people, I realized that they were just like me, in the same place and doing the same thing. I realized that I had something to offer them. I was already spending so much time around them, so didn't they deserve to have all of me there? More than just for work—for laughs, for encouragement, for all the things that can make work not just a job, but a gathering of friends. By being a negative presence, even though I kept to myself, I was making their jobs harder to do and making their time there uncomfortable. So, even without considering the *personal* benefits of being a good servant at my job, I owed it to my coworkers to give it my all.

I also owed it to myself. Being unhappy makes for poor service. The more joy you have, the more you have to give to others. If I came to work tired and worn out, then I wouldn't be my best. Nor would work be enjoyable. In fact, I'd be doing a disservice to everyone, especially coworkers, who would have to deal with having a team member who couldn't pull his own weight. A natural result of being good at what you do is being happy, which in turn makes you even better—and it leaves you wondering how you ever did it any other way.

Many of us were taught that *performing* in life is important, but we miss the experience of *living* life. Most of us were raised without knowing how to love whatever we do. School is a burden and chore for 12 years, then college is simply a means to the end of getting a "good job," and then that job is just a means to the end of retiring, and retirement is —what? Golf? Cruise ships? The History Channel? Then death? I'm sorry, but I keep having the distinct feeling that there's more to life than joyless labor done to achieve a state of no responsibility, no struggle, no movement—and, ultimately, *no action*. Entering each day with the whole of your being, withholding none of yourself in anything you do, living each moment, no matter how humble it may seem, to its fullest: This is the opposite of entitlement. It's surrender. To become the best version of yourself requires you to give up the version of you that you have simply come to accept.

We have it all wrong. We're trying to live a life that isn't *for living*. It's just a march toward some fabled idea, some brief "nirvana" that ends in death (but funny that nirvana should include so much medication). Where are the movers and shakers of this generation, the people ready to change their world for the better? We are a suppressed people. We lack fire, determination, and joy.

Ultimately, we are a generation lacking love—and unless we wake up, one by one, and resolve to *serve* people with our time and energy, we will continue to live bleak, self-centered, and truly empty lives.

Your Bicycle Shop

Most people know the story: In 1903, two brothers successfully tested a heavier-than-air flying machine. They flew. Their names were Orville and Wilbur Wright, and never before had this been done, but they did it. They did it, even though they had to run a bicycle shop to support themselves while working on it. They had to design all of their own equipment, including a wind tunnel, because no one was funding or helping them. They invented aircraft controls and flying designs that no one had ever thought of before—all without outside intervention or support (yet their competitors had government funding and full teams of scientists).

Did it happen overnight? Of course not. But what kept Orville and Wilbur going was their dream of flying. They saw a world where people might be able to travel through the air, and they loved it, even before they experienced it. And because they did, everything else they did contributed to their dream. Even their bicycle shop taught them a little more about mechanics and engineering every day. It kept them sharp and busy.

Working at Starbucks has made me a better writer. It's given me the work ethic I always lacked, social skills, and even some mathematical finesse (which, for me, is nothing short of a miracle) from having to make change and count inventory. What has your coffee house job given you? What have you neglected to see as an opportunity to learn? I'm not meant to be a barista my whole life. Yet there are aspects to being a barista that have helped my character immensely. It's not my primary skill set, but the skills I've picked up and improved have polished many of the "rough edges" of my personality, while leaving me hungry for the opportunity to pursue what I really love. My "bicycle shop" came to me in the form of a Starbucks—but now, looking at how it's all connected, I'm thrilled to be a part of it.

Orville and Wilbur flew because they knew that the bicycles in their shop were just as important as the airplanes in their garage.

PART 4

Coffee House Calling

There is a design, an alignment, a cry; of my heart
to see: The beauty of love as it was made to be.

Mumford & Sons

*L*ove lives in me somehow, yet when I experience it, it seems bigger than me. I feel a sense of purpose in it. Is love just a desire built into my body, or does it go beyond my emotions? Why does it feel like a "calling" on my life, nudging me forward?

I was raised in the Christian religion, so when I was growing up, I was told a lot of things about love, and, more importantly, about God. One of the most common—and for me, one of the most significant—was that God had a plan for my life. That he was in control.

But it never seemed that simple to me. I never truly felt like I was a part of something greater—until I worked at Starbucks. Until I accepted, and realized (almost accidentally), that the plan I had longed for my whole life, that "perfect path," was right in front of me.

In seeking to simply do what was best for my friends and to do the best job I could for customers of Starbucks, I stumbled into a spiritual experience—because that's what truly *serving* is.

"Servant" implies that there's a Master—a source of guidance larger than myself. It implies that the source of this powerful love is something outside of me, and that's what I started to feel. Even removing the emotions and looking at it objectively, I saw that an unseen hand was at work in my life.

It's only by an impossibly intertwined series of events that I was able to get a job at Starbucks… and—as I discovered working there—none of it was random or pointless; someone or something very smart had set it up. The skills and tests of my character, the particular location and the particular people there: It was all a part of it. God had his own intent and his own grand purpose for me. That's why, when I tapped into love, and in turn, serving, my life changed so fantastically. The "plan" I started to conform to was more intelligent, more complete, and more real than anything I could have come up with. God intended for me to be at Starbucks—and when this shattering realization came upon me, I felt *loved*—and that's what allowed me to freely love others.

I finally felt okay with where I was. Instead of nervous and restless, I was suddenly comfortable. Workers who love what they do become almost blameless; they're able to let go of their mistakes because people notice when they're giving it everything. Even if you mess up, others are usually understanding and kind about it. People are flawed, but it's amazing how forgiving we are when a person in question is totally open, and despite their misstep, they made every effort to do it right.

The more I served my peers and customers at Starbucks, the more I projected a peace that people noticed. Because I started to feel happy and "full," people wondered where it was coming from. A good servant projects everything we search for in others, and in ourselves. They awaken the desire in each of us to love, because in their presence, we feel loved ourselves.

Serving others made me forget about the troubles and issues I was having outside of work. I never realized, before this, how much I always brought my other struggles into the fray. In my thoughts, I would always be miles away, thinking about what I was going to say to a girl, what I wanted to do after work, or where I wanted to go on vacation. When I accepted the place I was in, my mind stayed with what I was doing, and to my surprise, I found creative outlets at the store —I started to think about how drinks could be made more efficiently, how furniture could be moved around for a better atmosphere, and so on. I found that I had a genuine interest in coffee roasting and processing, and I came to learn and appreciate the different roasts that are applied to coffee.

This gave me a satisfaction I can't describe. I was finding a "place" in my day job. My personality found a niche where I could be useful. Plus, I love coffee (that is, drinking it), so becoming well-versed in it was easy and a good conversation-starter.

"Work" became so much fun! It was hardly work anymore. When you discover the treasure of serving with your heart and soul, you have energy, and there's life in your tasks and in your conversations. The "you" that no one else can bring to the table is there, because you showed up with all of you. You'll leave happy instead of tired, satisfied instead of needy, and ready for what's next.

Not an Accident

We live in a world that contains a lot of pain. And sometimes, we don't choose that pain—we're born into it. What we often forget, though, is that much of our pain *is* chosen. Sometimes we think, deep within ourselves, that we deserve to suffer—or that being a better version of ourselves is just too hard.

It is absolutely easier to just coast by, feeling sorry for yourself, but it's a certain path to misery. Trust me, I tried it. I realized that if I wanted change, I had to start with what I had, and give it my whole self. Giving your all is making a decision that what you're doing deserves your love. Instead of trying to escape—like I did, like we so often do—look at where you are and ask yourself: Could this be where I'm supposed to be? If it is, if it's not all an accident, then treat it so. Humbly stand exactly where you are and accept the plan laid out for you.

Everyone wants to change their world, but no one wants to *be* the change. This is a call for our generation to rise above the apathy we've become accustomed to. So I say we do it. I'm tired of waiting for life to happen to me. I'm tired of believing that something or someone is going to pull me away from the mediocrity and the drag. Looking at my own life, and the lives of others, it's never someone else that brings us personal change. Truly lasting change comes from personal choices.

Though we each have our own struggles in life, we all share a common dream: to be the person we know we should be. Our greatest self! You might feel like it's impossible to be that person—but if it was, why would you have that dream, that desire, to know and to be the fullest realization of *you?*

When I stopped looking for the key outside myself and realized that God's "voice" was *in me*, already nudging me forward, doors flew open—doors I thought would always be locked. I found instant redemption for weaknesses that I thought would be weaknesses forever.

Thinking about changing the world leads me to conclude that I can't do it. It's too big. What could I possibly do that would change, or even impact, the world? It's a lost cause for just one person. But what I realized, working at Starbucks, is that there is something I can change: *my* world!

If I change me, then everything I do is changed. Every conversation. Even smaller things, like my driving, are different. To change your world, change *you*.

We can't even begin to understand the effect that personal change has on other people—have you ever had your whole day brightened by one cheerful person, whom you may have met by chance? Have you had a stranger tell you something that changed your life or your perspective completely? What if you were the person able to do and say the right thing at the right time to have that affect on people? Your treatment of others ripples outward onto how they act, then their actions affect the people of their world, and the effect continues onward. So who are you or I to say that what we do in a coffee house, or in the grocery store, or anywhere, has no significance or no meaning for the world? Who knows whom you may meet tomorrow, or what opportunities lay sleeping in everyday conversation, waiting for a good servant to wake them? I'm amazed at how much we really can do, at how much we really can change, if we just start with *us*.

Because we, as all generations in the past, have literally been given the world. It is our inheritance. Yet, we treat it as something we won't have until the future comes upon us. Don't we, in reality, have it today? Aren't we here? But given our current attitude, when the future does come upon us, will we be ready and willing to do anything with it, or will we just mess it up in a uniquely new way?

I asked "why" my whole life partly because it has all been done already. Many people just suffered through their coffee house jobs, and are still waiting. A lot of people made the money and got the jobs they always wanted to have, yet they're still waiting, too. We weren't taught to joyfully live life to its fullest; we were taught to look toward a happy retirement. Yet retirees also look forward… to their death. What makes me different? Do I think I'm going to find something different if I simply follow the path that my culture says is right?

No. But the solution isn't to run away, either. That's been done, too. No, there's something else we're meant to do as a generation. We in our multitudes are working on degrees we don't like, in jobs we don't like, and all the entertainment in the world just isn't enough to make it all right. To truly break out, we have to do something that we've never done before. In fact, I think we have to *be* something that we haven't been willing to be.

We have to be our best. And to be your best, to live and act as the ultimate realization of yourself, you have to *serve*. Would the best "you" run away from your life? Would the best "you" whine and complain that the world is unjust, and that you are a helpless victim?

Would the best "you" halfheartedly wait for a future that, according to your experience, is never going to come?

All I know is that the best "me" wouldn't. I may not have all the answers, but I know that life happens a step at a time—and how I take this step, today, affects the one I will take after. So, surely it's in my best interest to take each step with all of me—so that my feet land on solid ground. And what would life be if I didn't enjoy its steps?

Unless I have love, it's truly impossible. Unless I choose to get in and accept that love is in my life and stems from a source outside myself, I'll end up with what selfishness and entitlement always got me—a loveless, colorless, and joyless life. And no one wants that. Only by the force of love are great things done, like flying, even if a thousand people before you have tried and failed. The Wright brothers loved their dream, and they got to experience the impossible joy of achieving it. Unless they had been willing to give *everything* to their pursuit of flight, they wouldn't have succeeded. It's what set them apart!

Your "coffee house job" was given to you out of love. It's far from punishment. It's an opportunity to walk through the front door into the life you want to have—into the "you" that you wish you were.

When Is It Time?

I think I have found the reason "why" I should succeed at my coffee house job. It's not because I have some "duty" to do well or to please the people around me. It's not because I want recognition for being a "good person." It's not to make more money or to "advance" in the company. It's not even so I can move on to bigger and better things. It's for everyone else who works there, and for everyone who comes through the door. How anyone's day goes depends largely on how people treat them—so I have a choice to make for them, not me. Looking at them, even those I may not get along with, I know that they deserve me at my best. As I learned with Ben (who later became, for me at least, one of the best people to work with), people are always more than they seem. They're on the same journey as I am, so why don't we all give it our best and have a great time? They deserve it.

As anyone who has been "in love" knows, it's the best feeling in the world. And not only do I want that, I want to know its source. Feelings are fleeting, but a *calling* on my life goes beyond bad days and good days. I can't always get what I want, but I can flourish with what I have. My coffee house job is what I'm doing right now... and that's okay with me. Who am I to say that I'm ready for my "dream job"? Today, I have a source of income, people I can relate to and laugh with, and something to occupy my time that is all about serving people. And, honestly looking at it, it's enough.

I needed this. I needed a place where I could focus on other people. I needed to learn the meaning and value of honest, hard work and the simple treasure of doing a small thing very well. But working at Starbucks was just for me, for my life. What did God give you to work on? Do you work at a supermarket, a computer store, or a software firm? Do you wait tables or tend bar? There's something your hands are meant for today, and until you can succeed in that and be the *best* at it, until you are able to lift up the people around you without even trying, and until you can be thankful that you found joy in something you once thought was insignificant, you won't be ready for the next step in your life. My "coffee house job" isn't just preparation; it's the step I'm on in my journey. It's part of my life's work.

When is it time to give this life a good try? That dream you're waiting for is waiting for you, too. If you feel stuck and you're living like life is going to "happen" to you one day, then maybe it's time to look at that. Our lives shouldn't just happen to us. Despite your childhood pain and the wrongs you've committed or those committed against you, you were given a coffee house job for a reason—and it's yours to succeed in or to half-heartedly waste. What could you possibly lose by serving others? Only your pride. It all comes down to what you really want: love or selfishness? Revolution or implosion? Are you just a worker, or a *servant?*

A sign, or a wake-up call, is not a promise. I had to follow the plan laid before me, not make up my own, and this was the biggest lesson learned at my coffee house. I was not the master of my own destiny. Each individual day spent at Starbucks has been its own choice to make, and indeed, so has each moment, because at any time, if I wanted to, I could go back to feeling disgruntled and unhappy with my work. Yet every day that I've obeyed that voice within—those "instincts" and "feelings"—I've been able to genuinely want and do what's best for others.

It's that "force," "energy," or whatever you choose to call God, that keeps me giving my best, and ultimately, I can do only what he steers me to do, and I can only give what he allows me to give. Surely the master of the universe knows what's best for me better than I do—and realizing this is what keeps me from falling back into old habits. I may experience him as this energy, feeling, and motivating force within myself, and I may call that experience "love," but ultimately, that love stems from him, and is the crucial reason and motivation behind all things—which, for me, my life, and my little job at a coffee house, has proven to be beautiful, transformative, and revolutionary...

And I hope it can be for you, too.

DRIVE THRU

Revolution.

Acknowledgments

Thanks to my family for being supportive no matter what,

My roommates for hearing me out,

Elizabeth Solano for taking pictures on such short notice,

John and Sandy Lancaster for planting good seeds,

And of course, coworkers and managers at Starbucks—you are extraordinary people who deserve the very best of every day. I truly appreciate what it takes for you to do your jobs. My life is better each day I get to see you, and I am deeply blessed by having the opportunity to work with you toward a common goal of "inspiring and nurturing the human spirit." You are all there for a reason and I hope we can always find new ways to help each other, make our environment more enlightening, and effectively clean those oven stones... I still haven't figured out a way to really make those damn things shine.

Sincerely, with all of me: thank you.

Alex

www.ingramcontent.com/pod-product-compliance
Lightning Source LLC
Chambersburg PA
CBHW071937020426
42331CB00010B/2906

MALKIN

HISTORICAL NOTE

In the Pendle region of Lancashire in March 1612, a travelling trader collapsed in Trawden Forest. He believed he had been cursed by a witch. Following this accusation, four local women were taken from their homes in early April and imprisoned at Lancaster Castle.

On April 27, a group of approximately twenty people gathered at a house known as Malkin Tower. After this meeting, those thought to have attended were arrested and a further nine inhabitants of the Forest of Pendle sent to await trial.

At the Lancaster Assizes, between August 18 and 19, the Pendle Witches were tried. One of the accused – a child, aged nine – spoke out against the others, including her mother, brother and a number of people she barely knew.

On August 19, ten of the accused were hanged on charges of witchcraft. Another was also charged, and was imprisoned for a further year as a result. One more had already died in the dungeon. Only one walked away.

Camille Ralphs, October 2015

OTHER BOOKS FROM THE EMMA PRESS

THE EMMA PRESS PICKS

The Flower and the Plough by Rachel Piercey
The Emmores by Richard O'Brien
The Held and the Lost by Kristen Roberts
Captain Love and the Five Joaquins by John Clegg
DISSOLVE to: L.A. by James Trevelyan
The Dragon and The Bomb by Andrew Wynn Owen
Meat Songs by Jack Nicholls
Birmingham Jazz Incarnation by Simon Turner
Bezdelki by Carol Rumens
Requiem, by Síofra McSherry
Call and Response, by Rachel Spence
Lost City, by Roz Goddard

POETRY PAMPHLETS

Pisanki by Zosia Kuczyńska
Who Seemed Alive & Altogether Real by Padraig Regan
Paisley by Rakhshan Rizwan
Now You Can Look by Julia Bird

POETRY ANTHOLOGIES

The Emma Press Anthology of the Sea
This Is Not Your Final Form: Poems about Birmingham
The Emma Press Anthology of Aunts
The Emma Press Anthology of Love

SHORT STORY COLLECTIONS

First fox by Leanne Radojkovich
Postcard Stories by Jan Carson
The Secret Box by Daina Tabūna